Spotting Planes

Bill Gunston

Illustrated by
Geoff Hunt and Ben Simons

Gloucester Press · New York · Toronto · 1979

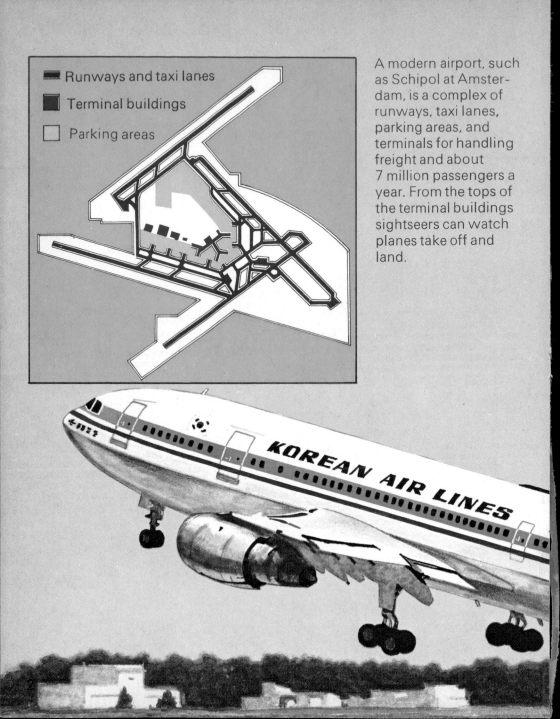

Runways and taxi lanes

Terminal buildings

Parking areas

A modern airport, such as Schipol at Amsterdam, is a complex of runways, taxi lanes, parking areas, and terminals for handling freight and about 7 million passengers a year. From the tops of the terminal buildings sightseers can watch planes take off and land.

Watching planes

The Airbus A300B (below) is one of the world's newest airliners. Seen here with the markings of Korean Air Lines, it is pictured just after taking off. In a few seconds the landing gear on the nose and the wings will fold away, and a little later the flaps on the trailing edge of the wings will also retract. Though very large, the A300B is one of the quietest aircraft in the sky.

Planes are among the most fascinating machines ever built by man. All over the world, people crowd to airports and airfields to watch them fly in and out. In large civil airports, there are often special areas specifically set aside for plane spotters.

At first glance, many planes seem very much alike, especially if viewed at a distance. With a bit of practice, however, you will soon begin to pick up their distinguishing features and learn to tell the various shapes of wings and engines apart. In time, even different versions of the same type will become obvious.

The main things you need to go spotting are sunglasses, a notebook and pen, and binoculars. Some people also use "aircraft band" radios to pick up conversations between the pilots and the control tower.

Recognizing planes

A plane can be identified in a number of ways. Close up, the company insignia and name, and the registration number will tell you everything you need to know to find it in a spotter's guide. At a distance, the silhouette of the plane and the number of engines reveal what type it is. Once you are familiar with the parts of a plane, minor variations are easy to spot too.

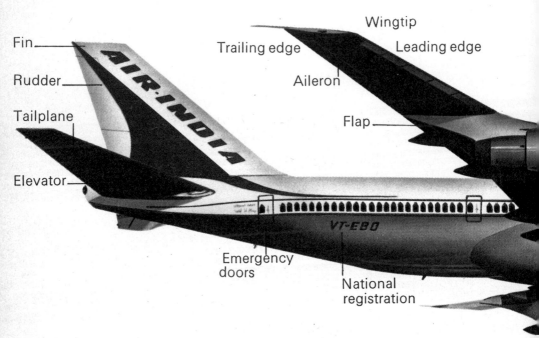

Wingtip

Fin

Trailing edge

Leading edge

Rudder

Aileron

Tailplane

Flap

Elevator

Emergency
doors

National
registration

VT-EBO

At the tail is a rudder that keeps the aircraft flying straight. The tailplane elevators are used to dive or climb.

On the trailing edge of the wings are flaps that increase lift at low speeds, and ailerons that are used to bank.

Engines hang beneath the wings from pylons. They are set in stream-lined housings called "nacelles" or "pods."

Most aircraft exist in more than one version. The 747, for example, can be fitted with engines by any of three different makers. There is also a 747SP (Special Performance) version for extra-long flights. This is a shorter plane and has a larger vertical tail section.

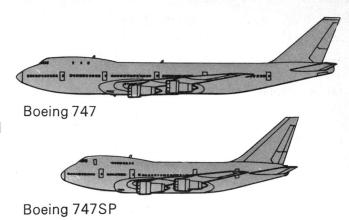

Boeing 747

Boeing 747SP

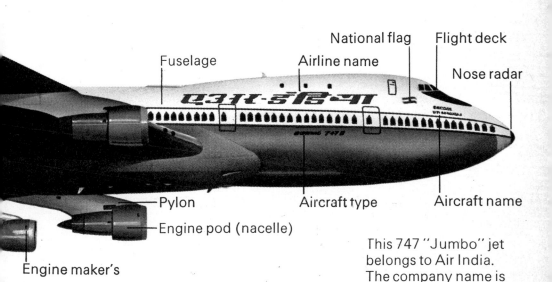

National flag

Flight deck

Fuselage

Airline name

Nose radar

Pylon

Aircraft type

Aircraft name

Engine pod (nacelle)

Engine maker's insignia

At the front of an aircraft is the flight deck. In the nose is complex electronic and radar equipment.

This 747 "Jumbo" jet belongs to Air India. The company name is in English as well as in the national language. The registration number must be visible from all sides.

5

Piston-engined planes

The heyday of the piston-engined plane has long been over although thousands are still in use all around the world. Until 1952, civil airlines flew nothing but piston-engined aircraft. Today, this kind of engine – which is very similar to a car engine but much more powerful – is found mostly in older craft or in smaller passenger transports. People still find them useful because they are cheaper to buy than jets and are easier to refuel and service in places that are off main air routes.

Why did airlines change to using jets? One of the main reasons was that jet engines were far more powerful than piston ones. It meant that passengers could get to their destinations in a fraction of the former time. Because jet engines operate at higher altitudes, they also allow for a much smoother ride. Modern jets also need less attention than piston engines.

The Britten-Norman Trislander (below) is an enlarged version of the 10-seater Islander. Seating 18, it has a third engine added at the tail. Its landing gear is fixed. Trislanders can almost do the job of a DC-3, but they need only one third of the power.

The DC-3, first flown in 1953, was for many years the world's most popular airliner. Thousands were produced, many of which are still flying on the more remote routes of today. The Piper Navajo is a typical example of a modern piston-engined plane used for private charter and as a business aircraft. It seats from five to ten people.

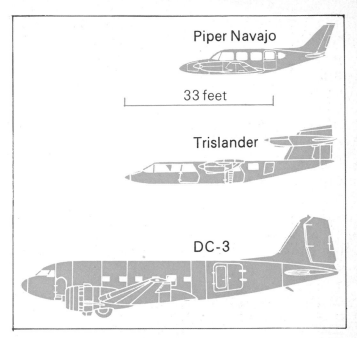

Piper Navajo

33 feet

Trislander

DC-3

AURIGNY

G-BCXV

BAe 748-2A

33 feet

Viscount 800

F27 Friendship 200

Jetprop

PHII

PI-C1015

Turboprop aircraft

Turboprops are gas-turbine jet engines with a propeller added. Compared with jets, turboprops are more economical but slower (250-350 mph). Most of the noise they make comes from the propeller, not the engine.

The Viscount was the first turboprop airliner to appear, going into service in 1953. Its engine, the Rolls-Royce Dart, was later used for such best-selling twin-engined airliners as the high-winged F27 Friendship (made in the Netherlands) and the Herald, and the low-winged BAe (British Aerospace) 748. Many are still used on secondary routes, often serving short, rough airstrips.

This BAe 748 (below) is a standard low-wing passenger aircraft. Typical seating on this plane is 48-58 passengers. The version shown here carries the markings of PAL – Philippine Airlines. There is also a version with a large rear door

Early jets

The de Havilland Comet opened the jet age on the route from London to Johannesburg on May 2, 1952. Today, only a few of the bigger Comets are left, flying holiday package-tour charters.

Far more numerous are the much heavier and more powerful Boeing 707 and DC-8, which have engine pods hung on swept wings and can fly long-range routes. Most seat up to about 190 people, but the final DC-8 models, called the Super 60 series, seat up to 251 in much longer bodies.

It takes great skill to tell a 707 and a DC-8 apart. Points to look for are variations in wings, tails, and window sizes, and the DC-8's down-looking nose with cabin-air intakes on each side.

This plane (below) is a Delta Airlines DC-8 Super 60. Delta is one of the busiest airlines in America. Most DC-8s were 150 feet long, but the Super 61 and 63 (known as the stretched versions) are 187 feet long.

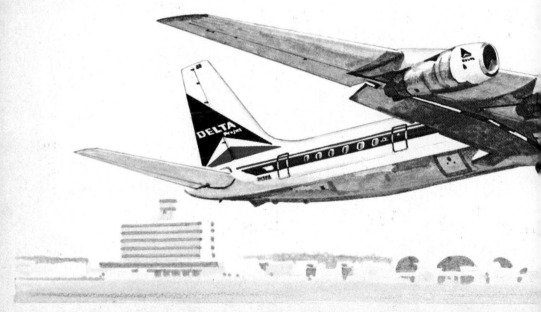

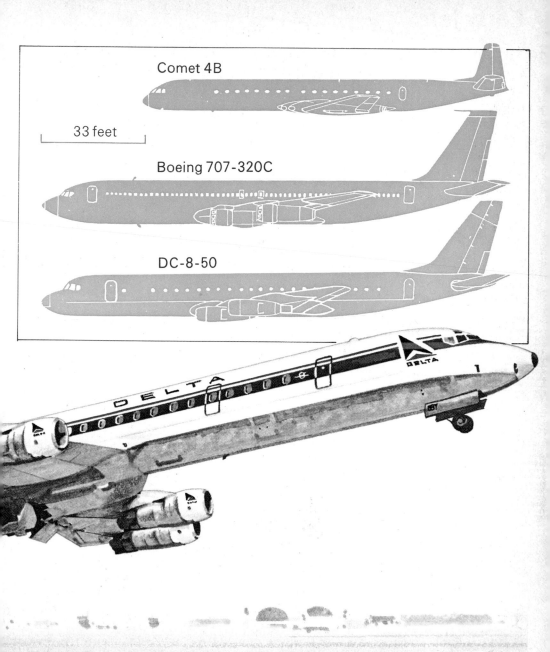

Comet 4B

33 feet

Boeing 707-320C

DC-8-50

Engines at the back

The turbojet made possible many new air-craft designs. The French decided it would be a good idea to hang jets on the rear fuselage of the new Caravelle, first flown in 1955. It worked beautifully, and the result was the first short-haul (short-range) jet that, contrary to the experts' predictions, sold well all over the world.

Caught napping, American, British, and Russian planemakers copied this rear-engined layout. The VC10 and Il-62 are long-haul airliners with four rear engines.

Though all three-engined airliners have at least one engine at the back, most modern airliners have engines under the wing. This can make the aircraft lighter and the engines are easier to get at. One airliner, the rare VFW 614, has engines in pods high above the wing!

This BAe One-Eleven 500 (below) belongs to Tarom of Romania. The One-Eleven is now assembled in that country, though at first many of its parts, including the engines, came from Britain.

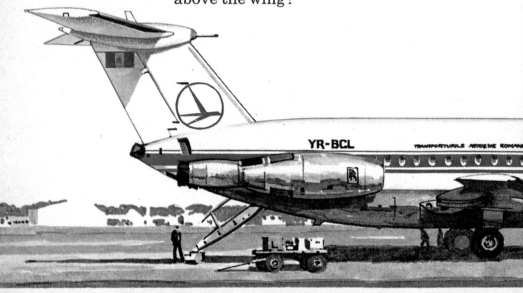

YR-BCL

TRANSPORTURILE AERIENE ROMANE

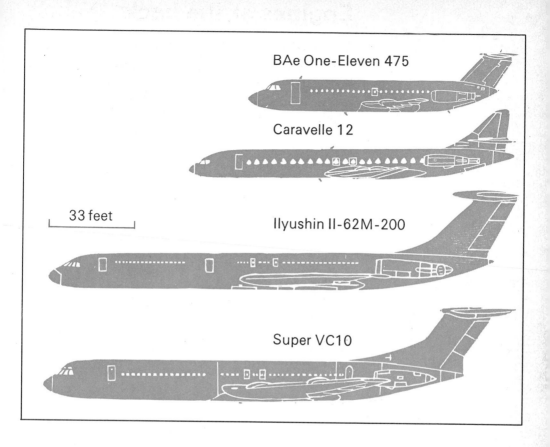

BAe One-Eleven 475

Caravelle 12

33 feet

Ilyushin Il-62M-200

Super VC10

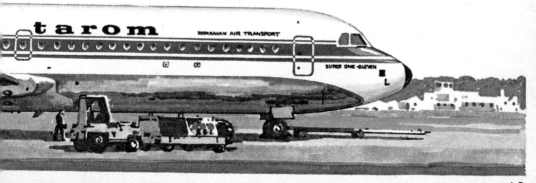

Modern twinjets

This important group of planes accounts for about half of the total aircraft movements at most modern airports. Twinjets are the modern successors of the pioneering Caravelle of the 1950s. They have much wider bodies and are fitted with quieter and more efficient engines, which are also much more powerful. This enables twinjets to carry more passengers and in greater comfort. However, these planes are still much noisier and less efficient than the latest generation of planes such as the Airbus A300B.

All three aircraft illustrated have turbofan engines. These are turbojets with extra-large "fan blades" enabling each engine to pump out a bigger, slower, and slightly quieter jet of about 15,000 lbs thrust. Two have rear engines and high T-tails. However, the 737, the newest, has underwing engines and a low tailplane.

The Tupolev Tu-134 is the Soviet Union's version of the modern twinjet. Early models were fitted with a "glassed" nose for navigation. More recent ones carry radar. The Tu-134 can carry up to 80 people.

The DC-9 (below), shown here with the markings of BWIA (British West Indian Airways), comes in no less than five different versions, capable of carrying between 80 to 180 people. This model seats 139.

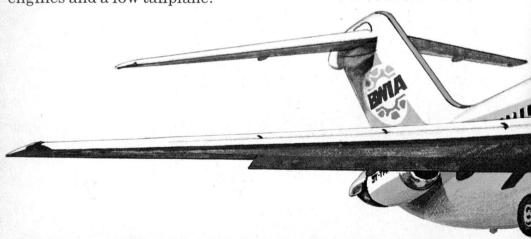

Boeing 737-200C

33 feet

Tupolev Tu-134A

DC-9-30

Trijets

Some of the most famous airliners of the 1930s had three engines, one on each wing and one on the nose. Jets made possible a new arrangement; this time the third engine is in the tail.

Britain's Trident was the first trijet. This very fast airliner exists in several versions, differing in length, wingtip shape, and other details. The big Trident 3 and 3B have a small fourth engine at the back to help during take-off.

Boeing's 727 is bigger than most Tridents and is the best-selling jet of today, with over 1,500 built. The Russian Yak-42 may be built in equal numbers for Aeroflot alone.

The 727 comes in two sizes. This Canadian example (below) is a long-body 727-200, seating up to 189. Today Boeing is planning to build a successor, the 757.

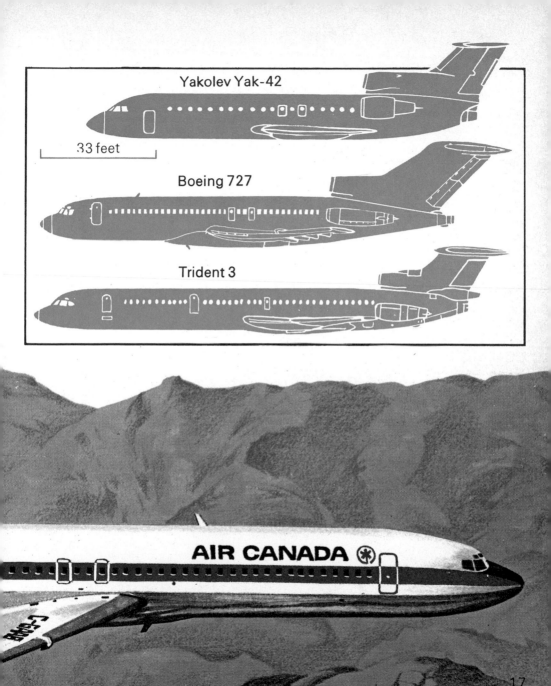

Yakolev Yak-42

33 feet

Boeing 727

Trident 3

AIR CANADA

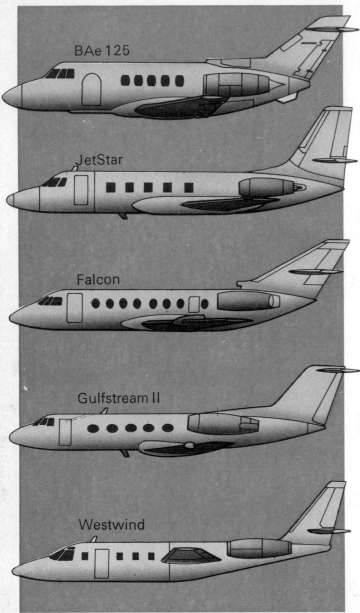

BAe 125

JetStar

Falcon

Gulfstream II

Westwind

Here (left) are some of the most numerous kinds of business, or executive, jets.

The British BAe 125 has the wing passing under the fuselage to leave the floor free from annoying steps.

The four-engined JetStar was the first "bizjet." Fuel is carried in tanks mounted on the wings.

The French Falcon 50 has a modern "super-critical" wing and three engines. It is a long-range development of the best-selling Falcon 20.

The big Gulfstream II has the same engine as the One-Eleven and the Trident.

Israel's Westwind has a mid-wing, without sweepback. Most business jets have a price-tag when new of about $2 to $4 million. Before one is bought, careful studies are made into whether or not it will save the buyer money.

Business jets

In 1960, nobody was sure the business jet, or "bizjet," would sell. At the time, big companies owned many aircraft, some of them cheap light-planes, some pensioned-off airliners, and some even converted bombers. The specially designed small jet would be wonderfully fast and convenient, but very expensive to buy.

Today there are thousands. Most seat six to ten people in a luxurious flying office where busy executives can get on with their work while traveling at 500 mph; there is no need to change planes or wait at airports any more. The "bizjet" soon pays for itself, and some big organizations own a small fleet! Most business jets look alike and the spotter can really test his skills on the differences in minor details.

The Rockwell Sabreliner 60 and the Gates Learjet 35 (below) are small but fast American jets. Both come in several versions with visible differences in the bodies, wings, engines, and windows.

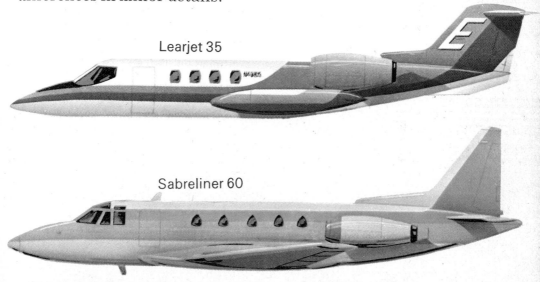

Learjet 35

Sabreliner 60

The Jumbo era

When the first Boeing 747s began flying the air routes in January 1970, people could readily see why they were known as "Jumbo Jets." Quite simply, they were the most enormous passenger planes ever to have flown. Jumbos can seat up to 500 people in a cabin that is 20 feet across, about twice the width of older airliners. Their take-off weight can reach as much as $\frac{3}{4}$ million pounds and their tails soar some 63 feet above the ground – as high as a three story building!

Airlines called the 747 the first "wide-body" jet. Next came the wide-body trijets; the L-1011 TriStar and the DC-10. Newest is the Airbus A300B, an advanced twin-jet aircraft made in Europe.

This 747-200 (below) belongs to El Al, the airline of Israel. Passengers sit on one deck, the crew on another higher up. A full-grown person can stand upright in one of the engine inlets.

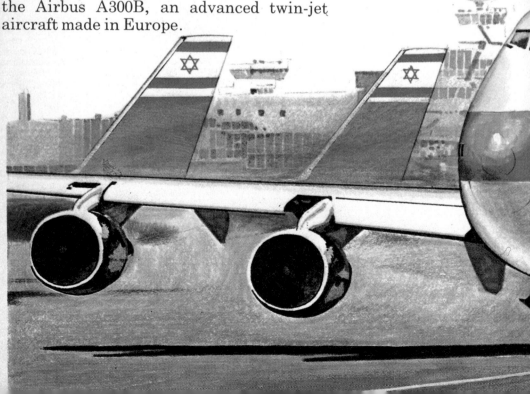

Boeing 747

33 feet

L-1011 TriStar

DC-10

A300B Airbus

EL AL

STOL aircraft

STOL stands for "Short Take-off and Landing." STOL aircraft are generally fitted with high, unswept wings and turbo-prop engines. Special high-lift flaps and slats (thin, extending sections along the leading edge of the main wing) help them to take off and land at very low speeds.

STOL aircraft are used wherever there are poor runways, or where airports are in high mountains or regions of very high temperatures where the air is thinner. They are usually rather slow (about 200 mph) and one of the most popular, the Twin Otter, even has fixed landing gear.

You can seat 20 people in a Twin Otter, 30 in the Shorts 330, and 50 in the four-engined Dash-7.

The Shorts 330 (below) belongs to the West German regional airline DLT. Built in Belfast in Northern Ireland, it is becoming a standard 30-seater "commuter airliner" all over the world. It is an extremely quiet plane both inside and out.

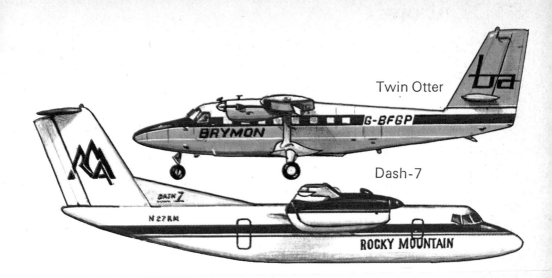

Twin Otter

G-BFGP

BRYMON

Dash-7

N27RM

DASH 7

ROCKY MOUNTAIN

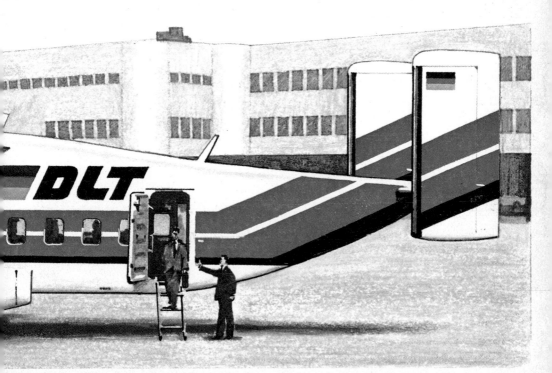

DLT

Helicopters

Helicopters cost more to buy and run than fixed-wing aeroplanes of a comparable size, but they can hover and land on small areas such as a ship's deck, or even a flat roof. The North Sea oil platforms all have "helipads." Other landing sites may be found on tall buildings in city centers or at riverside harbors.

Nearly all modern helicopters have turbine engines, making them far quieter and even safer, as they burn kerosene and not gasoline. Their small engines are set right under the main rotor, just above the cabin. The tail rotor keeps the fuselage from rotating in the opposite direction to the main rotor and also helps steering.

Most helicopters are either privately or military owned. Just a few regular routes are flown by airline helicopters to link airports with cities or to reach isolated places with no flat runway.

The French Puma seats 20 passengers, or can carry about 14 oil men loaded with their gear. The trim JetRanger has one engine and seats a pilot and four people. JetRangers do not have wheels but land on skids or inflatable floats.

The big Sikorsky S-6IN (below) is used to maintain a shuttle service between Heathrow and Gatwick Airports in London. It takes up to 30 passengers and is manned by a crew of three.

G-LINK

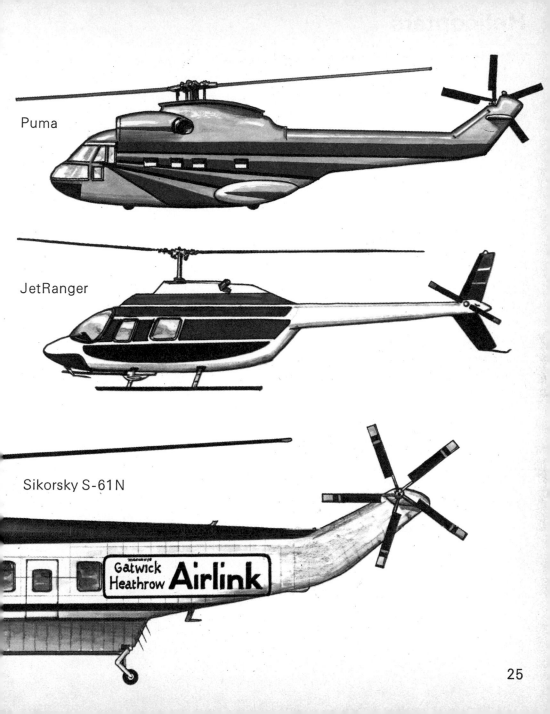

Puma

JetRanger

Sikorsky S-61N

Gatwick Heathrow **Airlink**

Spotting guide

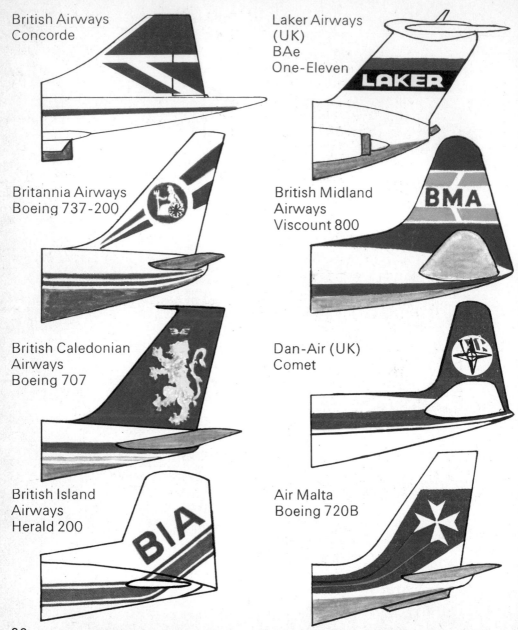

British Airways
Concorde

Laker Airways
(UK)
BAe
One-Eleven

Britannia Airways
Boeing 737-200

British Midland
Airways
Viscount 800

British Caledonian
Airways
Boeing 707

Dan-Air (UK)
Comet

British Island
Airways
Herald 200

Air Malta
Boeing 720B

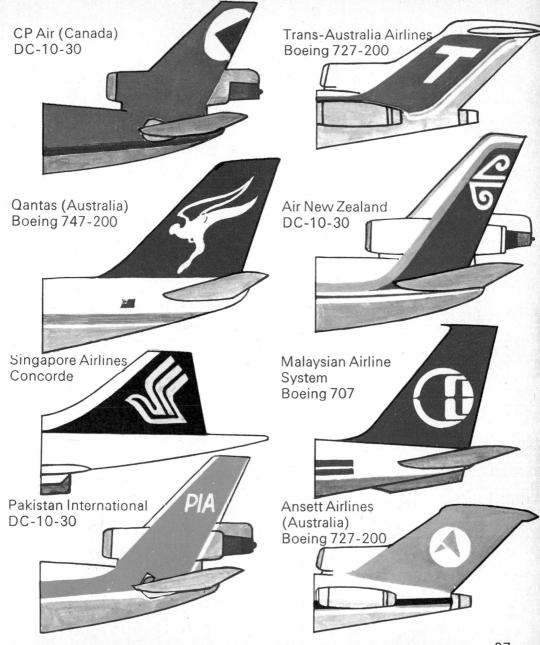

CP Air (Canada)
DC-10-30

Trans-Australia Airlines
Boeing 727-200

Qantas (Australia)
Boeing 747-200

Air New Zealand
DC-10-30

Singapore Airlines
Concorde

Malaysian Airline
System
Boeing 707

Pakistan International
DC-10-30

Ansett Airlines
(Australia)
Boeing 727-200

Spotting guide: Europe

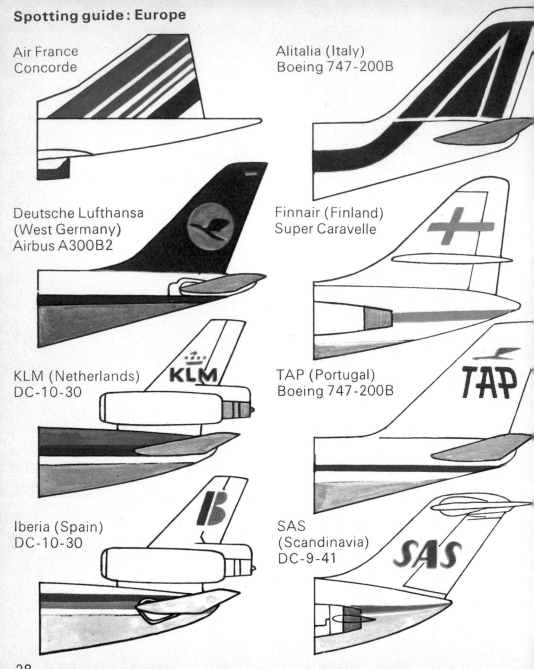

Air France
Concorde

Alitalia (Italy)
Boeing 747-200B

Deutsche Lufthansa
(West Germany)
Airbus A300B2

Finnair (Finland)
Super Caravelle

KLM (Netherlands)
DC-10-30

TAP (Portugal)
Boeing 747-200B

Iberia (Spain)
DC-10-30

SAS
(Scandinavia)
DC-9-41

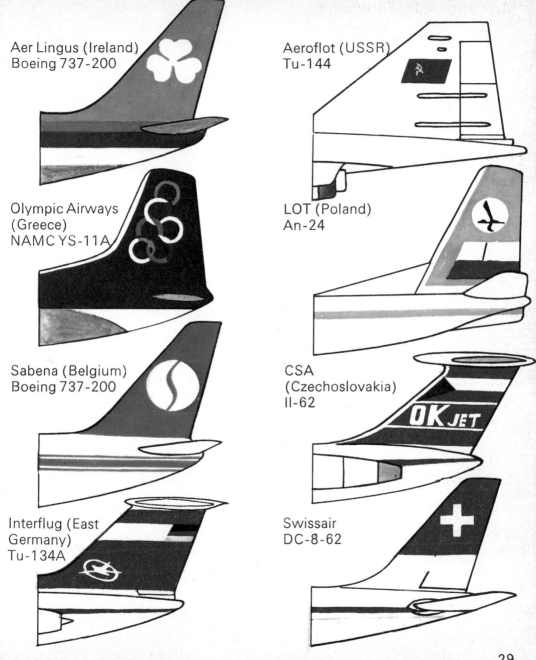

Aer Lingus (Ireland)
Boeing 737-200

Aeroflot (USSR)
Tu-144

Olympic Airways
(Greece)
NAMC YS-11A

LOT (Poland)
An-24

Sabena (Belgium)
Boeing 737-200

CSA
(Czechoslovakia)
Il-62

Interflug (East
Germany)
Tu-134A

Swissair
DC-8-62

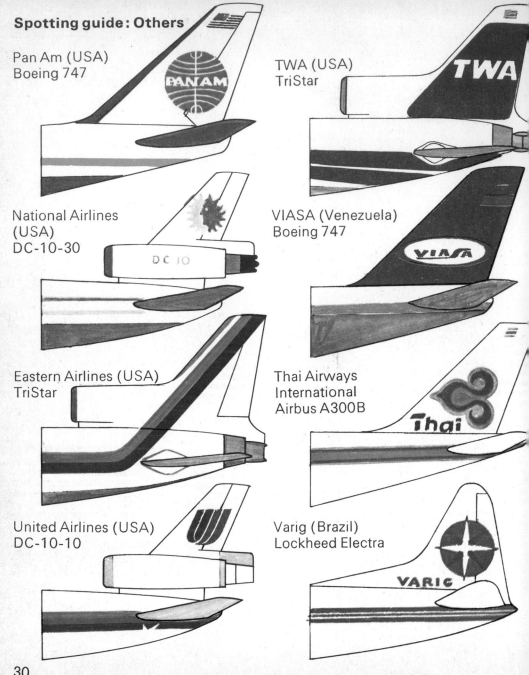

Spotting guide: Others

Pan Am (USA)
Boeing 747

TWA (USA)
TriStar

National Airlines
(USA)
DC-10-30

VIASA (Venezuela)
Boeing 747

Eastern Airlines (USA)
TriStar

Thai Airways
International
Airbus A300B

United Airlines (USA)
DC-10-10

Varig (Brazil)
Lockheed Electra

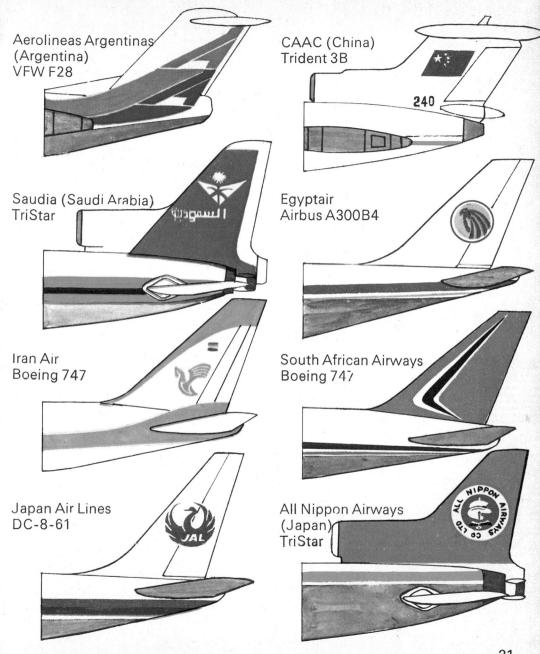

Aerolineas Argentinas
(Argentina)
VFW F28

CAAC (China)
Trident 3B

240

Saudia (Saudi Arabia)
TriStar

Egyptair
Airbus A300B4

Iran Air
Boeing 747

South African Airways
Boeing 747

Japan Air Lines
DC-8-61

JAL

All Nippon Airways
(Japan)
TriStar

ALL NIPPON AIRWAYS CO LTD

Plane registrations

Every civil aircraft in the world has a registration number ; just like the license plate of a car. The first set of letters and numbers tells the country of origin. The remaining ones identify the plane.

A2	Botswana	F	France	TJ	Cameroons	
A40	Gulf States	G	United Kingdom	TS	Tunisia	
AN	Nicaragua	HA	Hungary	VH	Australia	
AP	Pakistan	HB	Switzerland	VR-W	Rhodesia	
B	Taiwan	HC	Ecuador	VR-U	Brunei	
C	Canada	HI	Dominica	VT	India	
C2	Nauru	HK	Colombia	XA	Mexico	
CP	Bolivia	HL	South Korea	XY	Burma	
CC	Chile	HR	Honduras	YA	Afghanistan	
CCCP	Soviet Union	HS	Thailand	YI	Iraq	
CF	Canada	HZ	Saudi Arabia	YK	Syria	
CN	Morocco	I	Italy	YR	Romania	
CP	Bolivia	JA	Japan	YU	Yugoslavia	
CR	Mozambique	JY	Jordan	YV	Venezuela	
CS	Portugal	LN	Norway	ZK	New Zealand	
CU	Cuba	LV	Argentina	ZP	Paraguay	
D	West Germany	LX	Luxembourg	ZS	South Africa	
D2	Angola	LZ	Bulgaria	3D	Swaziland	
DM	East Germany	N	United States	4X	Israel	
EC	Spain	OB	Peru	5A	Libya	
EI	Ireland	OD	Lebanon	5Y	Kenya	
EL	Liberia	OE	Austria	5N	Nigeria	
EP	Iran	OH	Finland	5R	Malagasy Rep.	
ET	Ethiopia	OK	Czechoslovakia	6Y	Jamaica	
		OO	Belgium	7O	PDR of Yemen	
		OY	Denmark	7Q-Y	Malawi	
		PH	Netherlands	7T	Algeria	
		PK	Indonesia	8R	Guyana	
		PP	Brazil	9J	Zambia	
		PT	Brazil	9K	Kuwait	
		RP	Philippines	9L	Sierra Leone	
		SE	Sweden	9M	Malaysia	
		SP	Poland	9N	Nepal	
		ST	Sudan	9Q	Zaire	
		SU	Egypt	9V	Singapore	
		SX	Greece	9Y	Trinidad and	
		TC	Turkey		Tobago	
		TF	Iceland	(No letter)	China	